In a Promise

We are

In a Promise

Text by

HERBERT F. BROKERING

Photographs by

SISTER NOEMI WEYGANT

AUGSBURG PUBLISHING HOUSE
Minneapolis   Minnesota

ASSOCIATED CHURCH

IN A PROMISE

My eyes are awake
   before the watches
   of the night,
that I may meditate
   upon thy promise.

Psalm 119:148

Be seated

There was a place for man on earth.
A place of dominion.
The earth grew
and was in need of reaping.
God made man to be tiller
of sea and land and water and air
and of every living thing.
There were seasons
and for everything
a time, a place, and a person.
The earth was made
and there were high places to be filled.
Ladies and gentlemen were seated on earth,
and the world was in their hands.
Every thing in heaven and earth
was in their reach.
They did rule
and did present their high places
as inheritance to their children.
God made all things that they might be worked
and places to work all things.
Adam's work goes on.
Work is God's will.
There is work to do.

*God said to them, " . . . fill the
earth and subdue it."*

Genesis 1:28

Stop

God made man and man made fences.
Man said, Let there be a wall
and there was a wall.
The garden was a jungle.
Freedom was in bondage.
Faith was in doubt.
Knowledge was in trouble.
Eden was turned inside out.
The earth was barely dedicated
and already it was boarded up.
Man was out of Eden,
and there was a fad for fences.
Ghettos were the rage
and solid walls were style.
In the beginning
man turned the open garden
into a solid ghetto.
Adam, where are you?

*But the Lord God called to
the man, and said to him,
"Where are you?"*

Genesis 3:9

Repent

The plows were beaten into swords.
The farmers were steeped in war
and the ground was high in weeds.
Many plowings were over.
The soil lay still and mourning.
It was fallow early
and fed by much sweat and more blood.
Men worked less by the sweat of their brow
than for the blood of their brother.
Graves needed no tending
and there was no time for headstones;
nor room.
Sons of earth returned to mother earth
and she cried out for their peace.
Cain could not stand the cry
of the slain brother
and he abandoned the altar atrocity.
Cain plowed.
Cain plundered between plowings.
The steel stood still on holy ground,
where after worship
a brother arose from his knees to go to work
to kill a brother.
The fruit was on the altar.
The plow was left before the altar.
Life cried out of the sand.
Work was a weapon.
Cain could not do the creed.
It was a day for revenge. Remorse. Renewal.

And when they were in the field,
Cain rose up against his
brother Abel, and killed him.

Genesis 4:8

Begin again

It was time to begin again.
The Lord began again
and Noah came out of the boat.
He called man out of the flood and the deep freeze.
The people laughed and laughed
until they cried and cried,
and the water was taller than their fingertips.
Their chariots were heavier than the mire,
and their wheat was under water like refuse.
It was time to begin again,
and Noah and his family did.
Forty days and nights in deep water
and man began again.
The earth was void with flood and freeze,
and answered the call,
Let there be life.
It was the cry over the high waters,
over the smoking ruins,
over the waterlogged dwelling places,
and the thick red dust of the long dry desert.
Noah came out of deep water,
Abraham out of deep idolatry,
Jacob out of deep danger,
and Moses out of deep fear.
Adam was called out of earth.
God begins over
and makes out of nothing.
Noah, start over.

He blotted out every living thing
that was upon the face of the
ground. . . . But God remembered Noah.
Genesis 7:23; 8:1

Communicate

The sons of men were compartmentalized.
The house was a hotel.
The tents were separated by trenches
and high walls.
The property of the fathers was divided
and the property lines were greater
than the property.
The grass was greener on the fences.
The light was hotter on the fences
than on the fields.
Fences grew; fields withered.
The tents took refuge in valleys
and the hills became high mountains.
Gates rusted.
The people turned in cups to silversmiths,
who turned them into keys and locks.
The family had become foreigners.
Brothers were divided.
Language was multiplied.
Caves for shelter were dens for snipers.
Tents had become multiple dwellings.
The tribe had become a tower.
The people's thoughts had turned to babbling.
There was loneliness among the multitudes.
Pride divides.

*The Lord scattered them abroad
over the face of all the earth.*

Genesis 11:9

Follow

Sarah left all behind
and went with her husband Abraham
who went by faith.
Sarah left home
going over the hill
to the other end of the earth.
There was no use crying
over moving
what could not be moved.
Abraham was made for frontiers.
His heart was on the horizon.
Sarah's heart was with him.
Home was where Abraham could hang his heart.
Sarah ministered to her husband
and she served food to angels.
She left father and mother
and following the faith of a spirited man
she went west and east and north and south.
All she left did rust in her youth,
that she might follow faith
and bear a son in her old age.
She named him Laughter.
Isaac was her consolation prize.
It took a glad heart
to follow so much,
and leave so much behind.
Faith forsakes. Follows. Laughs.

And God said to Abraham, " . . . I will bless her,
and she shall be a mother of nations;
kings of peoples shall come from her."

Genesis 17:15, 16

Dig

The wells of Israel
had sprung a great leak,
and there was thirst in every throat.
Parched tongues murmured
and their words whined and whispered
and were in need of a long drink.
Forty days of rain
would have been relief;
they remembered the flood jealously.
The fathers prayed for sour water
and there was no sweet wine.
The currents were withered
and did not quench thirst.
The wells were desolate
and dry as the throats.
The people were out of water they had wasted,
from the wells they had let run dry.
They were out of wells
they had not dedicated and rededicated.
The people had skipped a thanksgiving.
There was one named Isaac
remembered for deep wells
and their water.
He dug his altars deep in the earth;
while some altars were covered with smoke
his altars were filled with water.
Wells wait for diggers.

I will open rivers on the bare heights,
and fountains in the midst of the valleys;
I will make the wilderness a pool of water,
and the dry land springs of water.

Isaiah 41:18

Dream

Men hunted and found.
Men rose and fell.
The boy was a runaway and a dreamer,
and God was in the dream.
Only ascending and descending angels
separated Jacob and Jehovah.
The earth trembled
but heaven did not fall.
The mountains shook
but there was peace in the heart of the boy.
He had pounded a rock and the ground
into a feather bed.
A nightmare was his vision.
Fear was cast out.
Jehovah had visited Jacob.
Jacob remembered Jehovah
and the feather bed of stone
became a cornerstone for a country cathedral.
Bethel.
The church was not arched
and it was not high,
for it could not cover so high a ladder
nor contain the land of the promise
nor outlast the time to come.
The dream was taller than pillars.
The church lay at the foot of the ladder
in the open.
Revelation cannot be confined.
It is very far and very near.

*And he dreamed that there was a
ladder set up on the earth, and
the top of it reached to heaven.*

Genesis 28:12

Forgive

Jacob had two wives.
Leah bore his children;
Rachel he loved.
Double doors were added
to a duplex household of Jacob.
He commuted within his own family
indulging in double talk
and traveling in double caravans.
The altars of Jacob
did double duty.
A twin had double-crossed his brother
and had inherited a double household.
Rachel died;
Leah lived.
The odds against Rachel's sons
were ten to two.
The tent of Israel had two doors
all his life.
Joseph was sold
and the odds were ten to one.
The wager ended in Egypt.
The father with his double cross
lived to see
the sons of Leah
place themselves as ransom
for the son of Rachel.
New doors were hung in the house of Jacob.
Come, Carpenter.

*Then Laban answered and said
to Jacob, " . . . Come now, let
us make a covenant, you and I."*

Genesis 31:43, 44

Be strong

Jacob's son Joseph was strong.
Far from home
he bound the wounds of the father's house.
Joseph united
Egypt and the house of his father.
He did bind
the grain bins of Pharaoh
to the empty sacks of Israel;
the rich pastures of Goshen
to the poverty-stricken herds of Judea.
He did bind Egypt's spansive space and time
to Israel's need for isolation
and four hundred years of time.
He did bring old Israel
to the birth place of a new nation.
Jacob was strong,
and all the armies of Pharaoh
could not hold the handful of his people.
They set their hearts to return.
So hard did their hearts beat
as to pull the chariots of Egypt down into the water.
Joseph's sons were strong
on the long way to home,
as he had been strong
on the long way away from home.
Faithfulness is power.

Behold, I have set you over
all the land of Egypt.

Genesis 41:41

Take, eat

The bread bins of Israel
were empty.
The shovels leaned like tired wood
and the sons were weary of weakness
in their fathers' work.
They wandered to the dry fields
and returned hungry.
They mumbled bread, bread to Jacob,
and there was no bread, for a while.
They would murmur bread, bread to Moses,
and there would be no bread, for a while.
Their bins were silent,
and their feasts forgotten
until the bread came down from Egypt.
And when the bins and the heart of Egypt
were shut
the feasts were silent again,
until the bread came down from heaven
like dew in the morning,
and like rain on the unjust.
When there was no food in all of Israel
there was plenty on earth.
The distance from Egypt to Israel,
and from heaven to Israel,
was the distance of mercy.
God remembered his people
and there was no hunger in Israel.
Israel returned to their eating places.
It was time to eat
and to remember God.
It was time to eat and to commune.
It was bread-breaking time.

*Moreover, all the earth came to Egypt
to Joseph to buy grain, because the
famine was severe over all the earth.*

Genesis 41:57

Be one

The household of Jacob
was rent in two,
and the ten sons hated Joseph.
The descendants of Jacob
spoke to Abraham's God
from two hills,
and did not speak to one another.
The lineage of Jacob
was lined up for war,
and the family tree was split to its root.
Two altars burned
and the high fences of borders
cast long shadows into the deep ditches
dividing them.
There was need for a new son
redeemed at the heart.
There was need for one
to intersect the thick cleavage
and to talk over the high walls
and walk over the deep ditches,
and to join valleys.
There was need for one to intersect
all frontlines
and to declare war on war.
They waited for one who would rend walls asunder,
rend thick curtains in twain,
rend graves open
and rend hearts free.
Help would come to heal the hurt
of a wedged household.
Breaks heal.
Scars are emblems. Badges. Signs.

Remember

Not gone and not forgotten.
They remembered their fathers and mothers.
They carried Joseph across the desert stretches
to the ground of his fathers
and the memory of his mother Rachel.
All the forefathers of decadent towns
lay like latent language
and silent stone type-set.
Green grass mounds and piles of stone
held on to biographic reviews for children's children.
Every marker was an abbreviation
of a very long story, not yet ended.
They piled stones where God had been great and good.
There was not room for all the words.
Earth could bear but brief inscriptions.
God's mercy was not gone
so long as it was not forgotten.
God does not forget.

*God will visit you, and bring
you up out of this land.*

Genesis 50:24

ASSOCIATED CHURCH

Move

Generations did come and go.
It was a mobile people
and God moved with his people.
There was no backlash in the heart of God
and there was no tent
he would not enter,
and no meal he would not grace.
The Lord stood before the door of Abraham
to save Sodom.
He stood inside the door of Lot
to save him from sodomy.
The Lord went before Israel
and behind them.
He was Lord of might and mercy.
He was guide of Moses and a nation afoot,
forming,
and on the loose awandering.
He was guest of king and leper,
and host to the harlot in the wall of Jericho,
and host of the high priest in the holy of holies.
Where there was man on the move,
there was the Lord
coming and going.
The children of God are on the move.

*You have stayed long enough
at this mountain; turn and
take your journey.*

Deuteronomy 1:6, 7

Good-bye

The honeymoon was over.
The birth cry of the first-born sons
was an echo at the wailing wall.
The heroes, hilarious on their furloughs,
had fallen on their knees beside breathless boys.
The laughter that had conceived sons
hung in the night
like ice,
and cold needles caught in a monotonous groove
at the very end of a lover's tune.
The lover's melody and hilarity
had turned to tragedy
and all oldest sons of Egypt's fairest women
were dead.
Seed was sorrow.
Once more was no more.
Good-night was good-bye.
The last plague had settled down
on a hot-blooded people
and a hotheaded pharaoh.
The testing of Moses' children's children
was settled on the tragic beds of Egypt.
Life was the price for freedom.
Egypt had a new list of mummies
and Israel had a new lease on life.
The cost for slavery or freedom was high.
It was a price that would not be slashed.
Life has a price. Freedom is expensive.

*At midnight the Lord smote all
the first-born in the land of Egypt.*
  Exodus 12:29

March

They walked over Jordan
and through the walls of Jericho.
The foot bridge of Israel
was safely suspended in a promise.
Pharaoh's daughter and Rahab the harlot
stood at the ends of a walk 400 years long.
A hungry family had migrated
with empty feed bags;
a nation returned
to milk and honey.
Goshen was past tense,
and Pharaoh's daughter saved a baby
bobbing in a wicker basket.
Jericho was current event
and Rahab the harlot saved spies
escaping down a roof top rope.
Courage reentered the stammering camp
and the people were articulate
in their walk and in their spirit.
Their songs were loosed.
Their march was full of cadence and confidence.
Their feet were freed.
The way over Jordan was like an iron road
beneath their rhythmic walk
and terrible trumpet tones.
The stumbling stones were stepping stones.
The children walked again
where their forefathers had fled.
It was a confident entry
and the earth matched the step of their spirit
and walls came crumbling down.
God's men go.

So these stones shall be
to the people of Israel
a memorial for ever.

Joshua 4:7

Soar

Hannah's prayer was lifted up
and in her old age
her spirit was caught in a whirlwind.
Her song soared
and happened
and was published.
Old Hannah and her new son Samuel
travelled to the temple
in the fullness of time.
He was weaned unto the Lord
and the holy place of the most high
was his bedroom.
The candles were his chores.
The high priest his guardian.
Samuel was a prophet in a silent generation.
The Word of the Lord was dumb
and the hope of the people was sentenced
to life imprisonment.
There was no new word from the Lord,
until the new son born of the old woman.
Hannah's song soared
and hung like hope
in all the walls of silent ghettos:
The Lord will make the poor into princes.
The Lord did the words of the song.
Hannahs are heard.

I have lent him to the Lord;
as long as he lives,
he is lent to the Lord.

I Samuel 1:28

Stand free

God had an old plan
for the twelve tribes of Israel.
They pitched their tents
in a new land,
and Israel had her heart back.
The tent ropes were long,
the stakes deep
and the houses were high.
God had brought his people out of darkness
and Israel stood free before her deliverer.
Her prophets walked the streets
like lamplighters,
and the judges like presidents before them.
The Lord was on Zion
and his will lay like a blueprint
in the words and works of the priests.
The mountain and the city
could not contain the will of the Lord.
It spread like dawn
and the God of tents and tribes
was on his way to the ends of the earth.
The whole world knows.

So Joshua sent the people away,
every man to his inheritance.

Joshua 24:28

Be strong

Samson had a secret strength.
The strength of Samson was a secret.
The power of God was hid in him
and his hair was a sign of the covenant.
Deep in the muscles of one man
was the power to wage wars
with a jackal jaw his only weapon.
His power was bound in chains for a season
and his eyes blinded
and his strength was laid in captivity
by Delilah.
Mighty Samson was a minstrel
and the weak made him blind
and made him dance and sing like a mime.
The power of God
lay like winter seed
in the sinews of Samson.
His strength was in slavery
until the hour had come for winter to go
and for the seed to grow.
The paralysis was displaced by power
ripping walls and pillars down
and the energy of the blinded Nazirite
let go.
It pounded people into rubble.
Samson had a secret strength
and there were the weak in need of his power.
Strength has a secret.

"O Lord God, remember me, I pray thee,
and strengthen me, I pray thee, only this
once, O God, that I may be avenged upon
the Philistines for one of my two eyes."

Judges 16:28

Silence

The bells of Mount Zion were mum.
There was no victory in the air.
Absalom did not win.
He hung limp and languid
in the air
and his donkey left him dangling
before the daggers of a general.
A traitor had skipped his trial,
and by his own doings
received the penalty of death.
Son, O son, O son,
wailed the voice of his father David.
Traitor, yes,
and a son was he.
The bells of Mount Zion were limp
and the heralds could not speak the headlines.
The news went through the land
like gusts of wind
and it had no tune.
Melodies stuck in the throats of the trumpets,
and all texts jammed
in the heart of the father
whose son was on the tree.
Royalty was refuse.
The king in waiting was bird bait.
David's harp was run out of alleluias.
It was in mourning and in waiting
for its next song.
Hearts can heal; silence can soothe.

And the king was deeply moved . . .
and as he went, he said,
"O Absalom, my son, my son!"
2 Samuel 18:33

Done

The victory parades were done.
Ticker tape was in the city dump
and the kings of Israel were on foot.
The princes were on foot.
Judah's kings were barefoot
and their soles were no more.
The wheels of chariots had ground to a halt.
Cheers had died down.
Parading and saluting
were documentary film
stored sullenly in the archives
of the quiet minds of old men and women.
The antics of all the priests had ground
to a halt.
Their doctrine was brittle
and dry
and their forms had no more life nor energy.
Dogma had lost its predicates.
Sacrifice had lost its subject.
Liturgical language had lost its voice.
Psalms had lost their vocabulary.
Story telling was for professionals.
The shadows were deep
and the day was dying,
and it was not done.
There were cut rates on holy sacrifices;
slashed prices on paschal lambs.
Offerings had run out.
The leaders of the Lord were under judgment
and their sterile congregations with them.
The fallen can rise.

*If you will not listen, if you will not
lay it to heart to give glory to my name,
says the Lord of hosts, then I will send
the curse upon you and I will curse
your blessings.*

Malachi 2:2

Wait

The king was gone for good.
Cattle had lain down in his temple
and strangers caroused in his kitchen.
His house was open all night
and all year.
Privacy was now open to the public
and the secret thoughts and desires
of Israel's king
were like city wash on the line,
like city scandal,
like a city siren.
The holy of holies was a stable,
and the outer courts like an anniversary sale.
The cattle were condemned
and up for public sale.
The oil of God's anointed
did not run over;
the horn had run out.
Saul had surrendered his sceptre
and the house had lost its good name.
The door was flung open
and none came
for the jealous king had failed
to show his people
the meaning of the door.
Stay-out had displaced come-in.
Unwelcome was written over the career of the king.
Welcome waits.

"Therefore wait for me,"
says the Lord.

Zephaniah 3:8

Be gone

The boundaries of Israel were temporary.
Old laws were feeble.
Israel had increased in stature
and in favor with God
and with man.
Israel could not be contained
in the vocabulary of the commandments
nor in the blueprints of the temple.
Israel was no longer a child.
The sides of the mighty crib came down.
Israel had a song for the world to sing,
and a spirit for the face of the earth.
She could no longer be contained in Sabbath walks
and bullock blood.
Israel's God was One
and he only had made heaven and earth
out of one word.
Property lines were obsolete
and the age of the ghetto was gone.
The towers of Babel and the division of the kingdoms
were old stories.
Fences were against the law
and its spirit.
Fences, come down.

*Great is the Lord, beyond
the border of Israel!*

  Malachi 1:5

Gone

King Ahab plundered what he coveted.
He took the vineyard
with the life of the vinekeeper.
He coveted what he could not buy.
He plundered what he could not pick.
He was a thief where he might have been an honored guest.
Jezebel and her accomplice
were struck
by the fury of the phenomenon of judgment.
The arbor had lost its luster.
The robber had beaten down the door,
and the host with the door.
Malice had turned to murder.
The door was down.
He was not welcome.
There was no one at home.
The way he took it
it did not belong to him.
There was no way to give it back
and no one to receive it.
Ahab was remembered for his rubble.
It was the last resolution
to which he signed his name.
They remembered Ahab
for what they tried to forget.
Coveting is a crime.

As soon as Ahab heard that Naboth was dead,
Ahab arose to go down to the vineyard of
Naboth the Jezreelite, to take possession of it.
  I Kings 21:16

Rebuild

The temple was on trial
and did hang by the nape of its neck.
The cedars of Lebanon
and the cypress of Ceylon
were to be hanged.
The jury was from the houses of the poor
and the testimony on the parched tongues of the thirsty.
Convicting evidence was in thirst and in poverty,
and debauchery.
The verdict would be given
by the imprisoned and the lonely
now in solemn recess to determine the outcome.
Love and charity
had been relegated to blood of bullocks
and stout incense
and golden seraphim.
The verdict was hard to hear
above the noise of those dedicated to
going on with the show.
The verdict was a loud and sudden
outcry.
The life of the bullocks was in the way
of the life of man.
The court could handle all the cases,
and there were cases everywhere.
Rigid thumbs went down.
Shrill voices went up.
The temples made by hand went out.
The vote was unanimous.
A new contract was in the offing.
Groundbreaking is underway.

O captive Jerusalem; loose the
bonds from your neck, . . . and you
shall be redeemed without money.

Isaiah 52:2, 3

Be redeemed

The laws were brittle and rigid
and Jeremiah broke them like a brittle yoke.
Elasticity had left the law
and royalty was rusty.
Nothing was new,
and the old was ready for the rubbish heap.
Flexibility had gone out the rulers' rules,
laws were turned to iron yokes,
and the iron was encrusted in rust.
Royalty had grown rigid.
Jeremiah beheld the weight of the weary
and broke the laws like pottery
and dumped them on the city dump,
in the presence of the leaders and God.
The dump was the altar
and rusted rules and sacrifice.
Precious pottery lay smashed in a heap.
Gladly the people unloaded
what had begun as spirit and ended as chains,
what had begun to set free and ended in slavery.
The laws were beyond restoration.
The spirit would begin anew.
The potter's wheel
was not stopped by the rubbish heap.
The new clay was warm and willing
on the wheel.
Jeremiah left the dump
and returned to the people.
Willing people. Warm people.
The potter redeems his clay.

*Behold, like the clay in the
potter's hand, so are you in
my hand, O house of Israel.*

Jeremiah 18:6

Ouch

Israel hurt.
There was pain in the people of Israel.
The lambs died for their shepherds.
Sheepfolds were emptied
upon the altars of celebrants,
and sin was white as wool.
Ouch was in the air.
Death had driven itself into the earth
and the walls of the holy city
were forsaken.
Silence reigned
and the people waited like barren Sarah
for the Lord to revisit.
Israel had been called
out of long night watches,
lingering flood waters,
out of much murmuring,
and out of enemy encampment on every side.
Doubt had hurt the spirits of men
and God came to call faithless to faith.
No longer would the pierced hearts of bullocks
suffice.
The day of vicarious incense was done.
The cry for shepherds and more shepherds was done.
It was a new day.
Sheep without shepherds were led
from their painful corners and crevices,
and there was peace in the valley
for a while.
Ouch is an old word.

For thus says the Lord God:
Behold, I, I myself will search
for my sheep, and will seek them out.
  Ezekiel 34:11

Be judged

It was doomsday in Babylon
and independence day in Israel.
It was harvest time,
and the wheels of God ground close.
Babylon was done.
God's visitation was a terror for Babylon
and a thanksgiving day for Israel.
Babylon became like stubble
and justice with her jury and her judge
came like a sea and a high tide,
and record-breaking waves were swallowed hard,
and the walls were like paper,
and their foundations like papier-mâché.
The tons of gods floated like cork
and the new shores were littered with
people and their idols.
Her mighty men of valor
were like wooden warriors bobbing on water,
and her bows and spears were like brittle reeds.
The city was cut to the ground
and her furrows ferreted with fire.
God visited the lands
according to the time of the harvest.
It was harvest time for tares and wheat.
His coming was judgment
or salvation.
God felt good for Israel.
God decides.

The daughter of Babylon is like a threshing
floor at the time when it is trodden;
yet a little while and the time
of her harvest will come.

Jeremiah 51:33

Be satisfied

He satisfied the thirst
of every thirsty thing.
He gave food out of every season
and with due meat he gave due drink.
The earth was ripe.
The cups overflowed.
The earth gave up treasures,
and caught the riches from the skies.
Heaven and earth were spread
like a bargain counter
before long lines of people
and what could not be bought
was free.
There was always thirst
and always the common cup.
There was no need
for travelers to die in thirst.
There was a cup.
There was a thirst.
There was a drink.
Deep water waited to be drawn
by new Rebekahs and new daughters of Jethro.
Water was sent for the thirsty
and the lonely,
to be given without price
to those
who would for a drop pay any price.
There is plenty.

Thou openest thy hand,
thou satisfiest the desire
of every living thing.

Psalm 145:16

Sing

Israel was in exile.
Like young eagles grounded
and their wings cut by strangers.
The youth were weary and withered
and their strength starved.
Their hearts were broken.
New singers had grown hoarse
and fresh harps just tuned
hung like old harness in dust,
and the quivering strings trembled stiffly.
There was no passion and no compassion.
The brittle bows bent like willow.
The hearts were broken from their dreams.
The exiled wept dry tears
and their prayers ran out.
They knew desolation
and the surrender for salvation.
Their silence was their only psalm.
Sagging shoulders was their exotic dance.
Their dance was seen.
The song was heard.
There are silent songs. Rehearsed.

Awake, O harp and lyre!
I will awake the dawn!

Psalm 108:2

Come home

The remnant waited
for the rest to return.
They returned
tempered in foreign fires
and trained in tears.
Their brittle manuscripts were like new skins.
Their history had been set to new tunes.
Their doctrine was now poetry.
Their confessions had become favorite bedtime stories.
Their declaration had turned to exclamation.
Their exile was the way home.
Information took on reformation.
They returned to do their fathers' dreams,
and to let out bids of contract
upon their fathers' blueprints.
It was a new generation.
They returned young
like pioneers
to break down the gullies in their fathers' fields;
to build walls upon their fathers' rubble.
The fathers were lost;
the sons were found.
The new day was like old times.
It was a new chapter of an old story.
The absolute end
found an absolutely new beginning.
God said there must be light,
and there was a new light.
Returning is a way of life; a doctrine.

*He will keep you in
exile no longer.*
Lamentations 4:22

Open

The law was lost.
Adam was the first to lose the key.
The chronicles of God
locked in the thick mortar of the temple wall
lay long and alone.
There were dry years in all the land,
and scrolls of Israel
were as locked as the Garden of Eden.
Scribes turned deaf and dumb.
Reflection and imagination were shut down.
The letter of the law was laid away.
The spirit lay down its own life.
In dry years
curious exiles on probation
dug into the rubble
and in the heat of the day
and the dust of the stone
the silent scrolls were struck
by picks.
There where men labored
in renewal and restoration
the Lord revealed again the law
with lock.
They came to read and hear and feed the poor,
and build.
They found the key.
Seek and find and open.

And the ears of all the people were
attentive to the book of the law.

Nehemiah 8:3

Surrender

Haman hung up his weapons,
he and a crowd of fellow executioners.
They swung on guillotines
and hung on their own weapons.
Esther was beauty queen for that day
and in the fulness of time.
When the contest was won
the woman of Israel was queen
and the wailing walls were still
again.
The laws for purging her people
were rescinded by the decree of her husband.
Israel was saved
by a heroine from a harem.
One by one by one
the insurrections ceased
and there was peace in every valley and Hebrew hill.
Tormentors were tried
according to their own deeds
and fair verdicts turned torture weapons
into artifacts.
Persian bandits were frisked
by the love and the creed
of a queen.
Israel could again walk and talk
and play and pipe,
and there was no mugging or murder on mainstreet.
Esther,
a Hebrew model,
was a savior.
The good wins.

There was gladness and
joy among the Jews,
a feast and a holiday.

Esther 8:17

Return

Jonah was gone
but Jonah would be back.
He could not stand the power of salvation.
The prejudiced prophet was at wit's end.
He fled on the way that comes back home.
Mercy lifted a city to her knees.
Mercy lifted Jonah to dry land.
God waited,
and Nineveh waited,
and the prophet waited,
and God outwaited the city and her prophet.
Mercy waits and waits and waits.
There was judgment on the land,
and the city was wrapped in sackcloth and ashes.
There was judgment on the sea,
and the man was wrapped in seaweed and mercy.
Mighty mercy was the miracle
outwaiting waiting.
Jonah came home.
Jonah went out to sea again.
Jonah will be back.
The prophets are out.

*Now the word of the Lord came to
Jonah. . . . But Jonah rose to flee . . .
from the presence of the Lord.*

Jonah 1:1-3

Be still

A strong wind blew over the family of Job
and there was no son and no daughter left
to tell of the terror.
The fields were stripped of herd and flock
and there was no estimate of the cost of the damage.
Job's property was plucked
and the east wind had no mercy,
nor did the friends
visiting with judgment.
A curse cut through their counsel
and raised havoc in a raging heart.
God's man was a prisoner of war
that plundered his possessions
and took his heart as bounty.
God heard the long furor
and the cursing chorus of his man.
When the storm was past
Job arose for rehabilitation.
He was a grey man
and he had a new creed,
and for Job, life began at eighty.
A rich man was richer.
God's man had found man's God
in hell, and in a hurricane.
Unbelief is cast out.

*Then Job arose, and rent his robe,
and shaved his head, and fell upon
the ground, and worshiped.*

Job 1:20

It's time

There was a time to plant
and a time to pick.
A time to weep, a time to dance.
God said there must be
the sun to rule by day,
the moon to rule by night,
and the man to rule both day and night;
and it was so.
The cold and the hot,
the wet and the dry,
the thick and the thin,
the land and the sea,
the seed and soil.
It was all so.
Conception and birth,
death and resurrection,
night and morning,
repenting and forgiving.
God made the cycles of all life,
all lines curved, beginnings and endings.
There is life in bending and refracting
of bent knees, bent backs, bent light.
It was not good for the dark to be alone
and God made light.
It was not good for male to be alone
and God made female.
It was not good for seed to be alone
and God made earth.
It was not good for death to be alone
and God made resurrection.
It was not good for the earth to be alone
and God made man.
God's word is life.

For everything there is a season,
and a time for every matter under heaven.

Ecclesiastes 3:1

Rise

Daniel dreamed of nations
of clay and iron and silver and gold
broken in pieces
and scattered like chaff in wind.
One by one they were crushed
and recorded in the chronicles.
The list of broken nations
read like a nightmare of memories.
It was Babylon's turn
and her hottest furnace fires
could not touch Shadrach, Meshach, and Abednego,
in the shadow of nations burned down.
Their hair did not singe
in the city where columns of stone on fire
turned to ashes
and where metal melted.
Candidates for fire and flame
were appointed rulers and chief prefects
in exile.
Dreams came true
and the three men tested by fire
stood taller than the ruins around them,
more remembered than Nebuchadnezzar,
king wonder of the world.
The kingdom of Daniel and its king
outlasts stone and metal and   dominions.
Righteous leaders, please rise.

*Then the king . . . commanded that Daniel
be taken up out of the den . . . and no
kind of hurt was found upon him.*

Daniel 6:23